Your turn to draw...

EDITION NUMBER ONE

This isn't your average drawing prompt book.

These artist prompts have been randomly generated from about eleventy squillion combinations, using subjects ranging from common household objects and familiar locations, to ancient Greek names and rare birds.

Get your mind working in a new and different way. Entice yourself to think of the obsurd, the weird, the absolutely wonderful, and watch as your creations come to life.

It's your turn to draw... what awaits your canvas?

Your turn to draw...
A HALF-MAMMAL-HALF-SAUCER

Your turn to draw...
THE CHIEF OF RIVERBEDS

Your turn to draw...
A COCKATOO, MINERAL COLLECTING

Your turn to draw...
A MOP IN FRONT OF A PIANO

Your turn to draw...

ARCHIMEDES, MAYOR OF THE HALLWAY

Your turn to draw...
A Butcherbird, petting cats

Your turn to draw...

ARCHIMEDES, LADY OF THE LIVING ROOM

Your turn to draw...
AN IMPORTANT BOOBY

Your turn to draw...
The Lieutenant of Streams

Your turn to draw...

A REPTILE MADE FROM PAPER BAGS

Your turn to draw...

A COMFORTER ADORNED WITH A MARKER PEN

Your turn to draw...
MASKS IN THE FOLLOWING STYLE: POP ART

Your turn to draw...

A HALF-FISH-HALF-SOFA

Your turn to draw...
A PREGNANT LEAFBIRD

Your turn to draw...

A HALF-BAT-HALF-CREDENZA

Your turn to draw...

AN OSTRICH, BLACKSMITHING

Your turn to draw...
A TALKATIVE APOSTLEBIRD

Your turn to draw...

A VIBRANT EMPORIUM. MUDDY FOOTSTEPS LITTER THE FLOOR.

Your turn to draw...
A TINY DEER

Your turn to draw...

ANDREAS, MOTHER OF CATFLAPS

Your turn to draw...

A TREE KANGAROO DRAWING A PORTRAIT OF A WOODPECKER

Your turn to draw...

A BOOKCASE ADORNED WITH AN END TABLE

Your turn to draw...
THE SENATOR OF SWAMPS

Your turn to draw...
A TRADITIONAL LOCKER ROOM. THE LIGHT FROM A STREET LAMP CASTS SHADOWS HERE.

Your turn to draw...
A HALF-PIG-HALF-CLOCK

Your turn to draw...

COAL MINERS HELMETS IN THE FOLLOWING STYLE: SCRIBBLING

Your turn to draw...
A Humphead Wrasse and a Shrew in the Pottery Scene from Ghost

Your turn to draw...

A DULL CONVENTION CENTER. PILES OF MAIL LITTER THE GROUND.

Your turn to draw...
AN IMPORTANT DRONGO

Your turn to draw...
A CARPET ON A CURTAIN

Your turn to draw...
A PHEASANT, SHOPPING

Your turn to draw...

A HALF-WOODCHUCK-HALF-MUG

Your turn to draw...
THE AGENT OF THE NEWS STAND

Your turn to draw…

A CONTEMPORARY TEAROOM. THERE IS A HUSTLE AND BUSTLE TO THE PLACE.

Your turn to draw...

A BISON MADE FROM LEAD

Your turn to draw...

A DOOR STOP MERGED WITH MODEL RAILWAYS

Your turn to draw...
A SPIDER MADE FROM IRON

Your turn to draw...

MIRRORS IN THE FOLLOWING STYLE: COLLABORATIVE

Your turn to draw...
A SNEEZING SWAN

Your turn to draw...
A TINY EMU

Your turn to draw...
A COMB INSIDE A PAINTING

Your turn to draw...

A MAMMAL MADE FROM INDUSTRIAL SLUDGE

Your turn to draw...
A HAUNTED SEA. IT SMELLS LIKE FRESH FRUIT.

Your turn to draw...

A DRYER ADORNED WITH A BINDER

Your turn to draw...
A SNAIL, GAMING

Your turn to draw...

AN AGGRESSIVE TODY

Your turn to draw...
A BOOK IN FRONT OF GEMSTONES

Your turn to draw...

A SNEEZING SWAN

Your turn to draw...
A SUNBIRD, HORSERIDING

Your turn to draw...

A GIGANTIC SANDGROUSE

www.ingramcontent.com/pod-product-compliance
Lightning Source LLC
Chambersburg PA
CBHW080602220526
45466CB00010B/3229